KU-307-837

Philip Ardagh's Shortcuts

A FAST
AND FUNNY
GUIDE TO

Queen Victoria

Philip Ardagh's Shortcuts

Elizabeth I
Florence Nightingale
Henry VIII
Julius Caesar
Marie Curie
Mary, Queen of Scots
Napoleon
Oliver Cromwell
Queen Victoria
William the Conqueror

Philip Ardagh's Shortcuts

A FAST AND FUNNY GUIDE TO

Queen Victoria

Illustrated by Mike Phillips

MACMILLAN CHILDREN'S BOOKS

For Héloïse, who IS amused . . .
Well, most of the time

First published 1999 by Macmillan Children's Books

This edition published 2013 by Macmillan Children's Books
a division of Macmillan Publishers Limited
20 New Wharf Road, London N1 9RR
Basingstoke and Oxford
Associated companies throughout the world
www.panmacmillan.com

ISBN 978-1-4472-4022-8

Text copyright © Philip Ardagh 1999
Illustrations copyright © Mike Phillips 1999

The right of Philip Ardagh and Mike Phillips to be identified as the
author and illustrator of this work has been asserted by them in
accordance with the Copyright, Designs and Patents Act 1988.

All rights reserved. No part of this publication may be
reproduced, stored in or introduced into a retrieval system, or
transmitted, in any form or by any means (electronic, mechanical,
photocopying, recording or otherwise), without the prior written
permission of the publisher. Any person who does any unauthorized
act in relation to this publication may be liable to criminal
prosecution and civil claims for damages.

1 3 5 7 9 8 6 4 2

A CIP catalogue record for this book is available from the British Library.

Printed and bound by CPI Group (UK) Ltd, Croydon CR0 4YY

This book is sold subject to the condition that it shall not,
by way of trade or otherwise, be lent, resold, hired out,
or otherwise circulated without the publisher's prior consent
in any form of binding or cover other than that in which
it is published and without a similar condition including this
condition being imposed on the subsequent purchaser.

CONTENTS

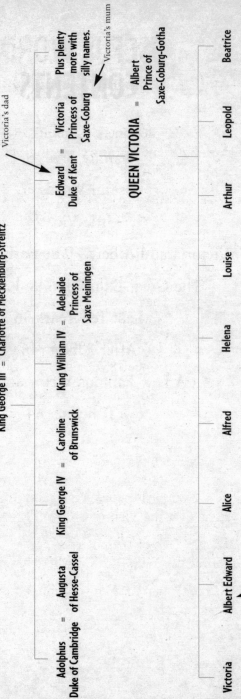

The Author's
FAMILY TREE OF QUEEN VICTORIA

without showing a single one of her horde of grandchildren

King George III = Charlotte of Mecklenburg-Strelitz

Adolphus = Augusta of Hesse-Cassel
Duke of Cambridge

King George IV = Caroline of Brunswick

King William IV = Adelaide Princess of Saxe Meiningen

Edward = Victoria Princess of Saxe-Coburg
Duke of Kent

Victoria's dad

Victoria's mum

Plus plenty more with silly names.

QUEEN VICTORIA = Albert Prince of Saxe-Coburg-Gotha

Victoria   Albert Edward   Alice   Alfred   Helena   Louise   Arthur   Leopold   Beatrice

"Bertie"

USEFUL WORDS
(and some not so useful ones too)

Ascot A horse race meeting in Ascot, Berkshire. 'Royal Ascot' (a four-day race meeting in June) was – and is – attended by royalty.

Boer War Nothing to do with bristly pigs (those were boars). Actually two wars: one in 1880-81 and one in 1899-1902, with the British against the Boers. Boers were descendants of Dutch and Huguenot colonists in South Africa.

British Empire The parts of the world claimed and governed by the British. Shown in red on Victorian maps.

Buckingham Palace The official town residence of the British monarch since 1837.

Chloroform An early form of anaesthetic. Poured on a cloth and held to your face it could knock you out. (Doctors first tried it out on themselves in 1847.)

Emigration Leaving your native country to set up a new home and start a new life abroad. Millions – yup, millions – of Irish and English people emigrated to the United States and Canada during Victoria's reign.

Eton The poshest of the posh fee-paying schools in Britain, named after the town of Eton where it's situated.

Fenian A member of a revolutionary group fighting for Ireland's freedom.

Flimp A Victorian purse-snatcher.

Illegitimate An illegitimate child was a child whose parents weren't married. They often didn't have the same rights as children who weren't illegitimate.

The Mall The long, straight road leading from Buckingham Palace to Trafalgar Square.

Mourning A period of grieving after someone has died.

Mudlarks People – usually young boys and old women – who collected coal from the Thames's river banks when the tide was out, then sold it.

Transportation Forced emigration. Forcing people from their native country and transporting them to another.

Typhoid A highly contagious disease which was good at killing members of royal families throughout Europe.

LITTLE VIC

Ask people to describe what Queen Victoria looked like and most of them will probably come up with a grumpy, little old lady – maybe a bit overweight – dressed in black, with her mouth turned down at the corners. Ask them to quote one of her most famous sayings, and they're likely to say: 'We are not amused.' The 'we' was a 'royal we' and simply meant 'I'. What she wasn't amused about is unimportant. It probably wasn't very funny anyway. What's interesting, though, is that this 'old' image is how most of us picture a queen who actually came to the throne when she was just eighteen years old.

HOMEWARD BOUND

Victoria hadn't been born to be queen, even though her father, the Duke of Kent, had got it into his head that his (then unborn) child would one day be a great ruler. Why? Because a Maltese gypsy had said so, and he took the prediction seriously – so seriously, in fact, that he drove his pregnant wife (the Duchess) on a bumpy coach across Germany and France. The Duke felt that a future king or queen should be born on English soil, and he was doing the driving because they couldn't afford a driver.

DAD'S AN EMBARRASSMENT

Victoria's father, the Duke, was once described as being 'the greatest rascal that ever went unhung'. (It should, of course, have been 'unhanged'... but you get the idea.) At one time, he was said to be the most hated man in the British army. Then as a young(ish) man, he was thrown out of it. He couldn't be bothered to work for a living so moved to Brussels where he thought it would be cheaper!

BUNDLE OF JOY

Victoria was born on 24 May 1819 at Kensington Palace. The reason why she was born in a palace was that she was the granddaughter of 'Mad' King George III, originally from Hanover in Germany. (The British royal family was not so British!) In other words, her father was one of George III's sons. As well as being Duke of Kent he was also a prince: Prince Edward. Two of George III's other sons were later to become George IV and William IV. So, although Victoria wasn't directly in line for the throne, she did have royal blood.

GOING, GOING, GONE

The Duke's two brothers (Victoria's uncles George IV and William IV) had thirteen children between them, all of whom would have been in line for the throne before Victoria, if it wasn't for two important reasons. They were either dead (so they couldn't rule) or were illegitimate (see page 8) so they weren't allowed to rule. That would have left her father as next in line, if he hadn't gone and died too . . . but more about that later.

THE NAME GAME

Victoria's christening took place at Kensington Palace on 24 June 1819. Two godfathers were chosen: Alexander I, the Tsar of Russia, and Victoria's uncle, the Prince Regent (later George IV). The Duke wanted to call his daughter Georgiana Charlotte Augusta Alexandrina Victoria. The 'Georgiana' was the female version of 'George' and 'Alexandrina' of 'Alexander'. The day before the event, the Prince Regent let it be known that he didn't approve of the name Georgiana. Why? Because if it went before Alexandrina that would be an insult to the Tsar. And, if it went after Alexandrina it would be an insult to him! To get his own back, the Duke simply called her 'Alexandrina' after the Tsar and, at the Prince Regent's insistence, plain old 'Victoria', after the girl's mother, the Duchess.

YOU WANT TO CALL HER 'VICTORIA'? WHAT GAVE YOU THAT RIDICULOUS IDEA?

IT'S MY NAME!

EARLY DAYS

For much of her childhood, therefore, Victoria was actually called 'Drina', a shortened version of her first name. For about the first three years of her life, she only spoke German. Then she started to learn English and French. Some royals and royal officials thought the names sounded too foreign. The British were still getting used to the idea of being ruled by the Hanoverians and didn't need their noses rubbed in it.

THREE BECOME TWO

In December 1819, when little Victoria – still being called Drina – was just six months or so old, she and her family went to stay in a cottage in Devon. They were there as guests of the Bishop of Salisbury, and stopped off to look around Salisbury cathedral along the way. There, Victoria's father, the Duke, caught a terrible cold. It was so terrible, in fact, that he died from it on 23 January 1820. His last words to his wife, the Duchess, were, 'Don't forget me'.

IN DIRE STRAITS

Victoria's father was buried in the royal vault at Windsor. This took place at night and the bulky coffin somehow got jammed in the entrance to the vault . . . but this was nothing compared to the jam he left his wife and daughter in. All the Duke had left them was debt. It was only thanks to Victoria's maternal uncle (her mother's brother, Prince Leopold) that the baby princess and the Duchess could even afford to stay on in England and Kensington Palace! Leopold then generously agreed to give them £2,000 a year. Later, when he could afford it, he raised this to £3,000. Thanks to him, the Duchess could now afford a nurse for Victoria, and other staff. From age five onwards, Victoria had a governess with the grand name of Baroness Louise Lehzen.

PETS AND DOLLS

From an early age, Victoria liked dolls and animals. Her mother had a pet canary and parakeet which Victoria loved, but her greatest affection was for the Duchess's King Charles spaniel, Dash. Victoria 'adopted' the dog and, when he died aged ten, Dash was buried in a very fine grave. Throughout her long life, Victoria had everything from Persian cats and all kinds of dogs – though she was particularly partial to collies for a while – to pigeons. She was also very fond of horses.

PIANO PLAYING? NIL POINTS.

As a girl, Princess Victoria loved learning languages. She was good at them. She enjoyed German – it was her mother tongue, remember – as well as French and Italian, but didn't like Latin at all. She loved singing and had a very good singing voice. John Sale, from St Margaret's Church,

14

Westminster, started giving her singing lessons when she was seven. She also learned drawing and dancing, which she really enjoyed. Piano lessons were less successful. When her piano teacher told her, 'You must practise like everyone else,' she slammed the piano lid. 'There!' she replied. 'You see there is no *must* about it.'

A FEW STEPS FROM THE THRONE

In March 1830, Victoria made an interesting discovery. She found a piece of paper slipped into her history book. It was the British monarchy's family tree, and most of the people on it were dead, except for her two uncles, King George IV and William . . . and herself. Then the truth must have dawned. Victoria was second in line to the throne. The story goes that she said to her governess, 'I am nearer to the throne than I thought,' then added the words, 'I will be good.' Well behaved? Good at lessons? Good as a ruler of Britain? Who knows. Three months later, the king died and her one remaining uncle, William, became king. Unless he had an heir, Victoria was now *first* in line for the crown of Great Britain!

MISSING ALL THE FUN

The Duchess of Kent realized just what an important person her daughter, Princess Victoria, had become, and she wanted everyone to know it. The new king was to be crowned on 3 September 1831 and he wanted his niece to be there, but the Duchess would have none of it. The order of the procession was worked out so that a whole load of royal dukes would follow the king, and Victoria would follow them. The Duchess argued that Victoria should be immediately behind her uncle and, if that wasn't possible, her daughter wouldn't be going at all. The sobbing Victoria had to make do with watching the procession from Marlborough House, instead of being a part of it.

THE KING IS DEAD. GOD SAVE THE QUEEN!

King William IV died early on the morning of 20 June 1837, which meant that Drina (young Vic) must be given the news. The Archbishop of Canterbury, the Lord Chamberlain and the late king's physician (doctor) nipped around to Kensington Palace to tell her. It was five o'clock in the morning and everyone was asleep, until the banging on the door woke the servants. They then woke Victoria's mum, the Duchess, who refused to fetch her daughter, explaining that – surprise, surprise – she was sleeping! The Duchess only agreed to get Victoria up when the visitors gave a strong hint as to what they were there for. They explained that they must see THE QUEEN . . . Q-U-E-E-N, geddit? The Duchess got it. Her daughter had only been a princess when she'd gone to bed.

YOUR CRUMPLED MAJESTY

Victoria didn't appear at her first engagement as queen in pomp and ceremony and finery, but in her nightie, dressing-gown and slippers. The three officials who'd come to Kensington Palace knelt before their new monarch, kissing her hand in turn, and told her of King William's death. According to her own journal (which is like a diary but nothing like a dairy), Victoria had a little cry for her dead uncle, then went to her room and got dressed. On 21 June 1837, Victoria was proclaimed queen to the crowds gathered outside St James's Palace. She was announced as 'Queen Alexandrina Victoria', but that was for the first and last time. The new queen made it perfectly clear that the name 'Alexandrina' was to be dropped and that she'd be known as 'Queen Victoria' from that moment on.

PUTTING MUM IN HER PLACE

Now that Victoria was queen, she was going to let her mum know who was boss. After all the Duchess had done to push her forward into public prominence, Victoria was going to push HER to one side. There were going to be plenty of changes around there. Up until then, they'd both been sleeping in the same room! Victoria ordered that the Duchess's bed be put somewhere else. By the time they'd all moved to Buckingham Palace, Victoria had given strict instructions that her mother be made to live in a distant wing of the palace, in her own suite of apartments, as far away from her as possible. This was done and the Duchess soon gained a reputation for being a grumpy old biddy who was always shouting at the servants.

THE CROWNING GLORY

Just over a year passed before Victoria's coronation. It was to be held at Westminster Abbey on 28 June 1838. (In other words, she was queen from the moment her uncle died, but wouldn't get to wear the crown until then.) A staggering £200,000 was spent on the event, which is still a lot of money today but would have been a *huge* amount back then. This was four times more than had been spent on William IV's coronation. The abbey was decked out in crimson and gold, there were fireworks displays and band concerts in every royal park and, at Hyde Park in London, there was a two-day festival of celebration.

THE QUEEN'S WEATHER

The day came, and there was glorious sunshine. Victoria got up at seven, but hadn't slept too well, what with all the music and cheerful shouting and the cannons being fired in

Hyde Park at 4.00 a.m.! By ten o'clock she was in the State Coach and on her way to the abbey, watched by crowds of over half a million people. Earlier that day, it had been raining but, now that the queen was out and about, the sun shone down. Nothing could spoil the great occasion . . . and sunshine became known as the 'Queen's Weather'.

A COMICAL CORONATION

Queen Victoria's coronation was a bit of a shambles! Two of those carrying the long train of Victoria's coronation robe chatted throughout. The Bishop of Bath and Wells turned over two pages of the order of service at once, so told her that it was finished when it hadn't . . . so he had to call the queen back! When Victoria entered St Edward's Chapel, she was amazed to find that wine and sandwiches had been left our for guests . . . on the ALTAR. And when it came to the Archbishop of Canterbury 'slipping' a ruby ring onto her finger, he forced it onto the wrong one. She only managed to get it off later, after bathing her hand in iced water!

THE REMARKABLE MR MICKLETHWAITE

As a part of the coronation celebrations, Queen Victoria published a list of Coronation Honours, granting certain people awards and titles. A Mr Peckham Micklethwaite of Sussex was created a lord (a baronet) for a most unusual reason . . . for sitting on the head of a runaway horse! Let me explain. During a 'Royal Progress' to St Leonards-on-Sea (which isn't that far from where I live, by the way), their carriage overturned and one of the horses broke free, chasing after the then Princess Victoria, her mother, her governess, and her mother's lady-in-waiting Lady Flora Hastings. Whilst they clambered over a wall to safety, Mr Micklethwaite managed to stop the horse and sit on its head! Such bravery was not forgotten.

A PRIME MOVER

Queen Victoria's first prime minister was a man called William Lamb, the Viscount Melbourne, but was better known as Lord Melbourne. He'd been prime minister for three years when Victoria became queen and was 58 years old (which was 40 years older than she was). They got on well together . . . *so* well, in fact, that people started calling Victoria 'Mrs Melbourne' behind her back! She was even hissed at by the crowd when she appeared at Ascot. News of this right royal rumour soon reached the palace's ears – and I'll bet you didn't know that the palace had ears – and it was decided that a suitable husband should be found for the queen.

THE BATTLE OF HASTINGS

The royal family needed to avoid scandal at all costs. There had already been a big to-do since Victoria came to the throne. In 1839, her mother, the Duchess of Kent had a lady-in-waiting called Lady Flora Hastings. When Lady Flora's tummy swelled up, the queen's doctor, Sir James Clark, gave her pills containing rhubarb. When these did nothing to help, he pronounced that the woman must be pregnant (the rumour was that the father was the Duchess of Kent's 'friend', Sir John Conroy). Lady Flora protested that this wasn't true and she couldn't be pregnant . . . and she battled to prove her innocence. Even Victoria didn't believe her. By the time Flora had proved it – thanks to another Doctor Clarke (Sir Charles Clarke, with an 'e') – it was too late. The swelling had been caused by cancer of the liver, and it killed her. But that wasn't an end to the gossip. Rumours soon spread that Lady Flora *had* been pregnant and had been killed to avoid a scandal!

SIR JAMES CLARK

Sir James Clark was both Queen Victoria and her mother's doctor, though it seems extraordinary that he ever got the job. He was really a naval doctor and a fresh-air freak. A Scot, he thought that fresh air was the answer to just about anything and everything. He even suggested that Buckingham Palace be pumped full of air because he was convinced that the trees surrounding it were clogging up the atmosphere. He almost succeeded in getting his fellow fresh-air freak Dr Arnott involved in work in the palace, until it was discovered that Arnott thought that a person could and would probably live for hundreds of years if only he or she got enough air! When Victoria caught typhoid, Sir James Clark wrongly diagnosed her as 'being bilious' (having indigestion) ... so his misdiagnosis of poor Lady Flora Hastings can't have come as a total surprise!

THANK YOU, SIR JAMES. I THINK THAT'S QUITE ENOUGH FRESH AIR FOR ONE DAY!

A CHOICE OF HUSBANDS

Eager to avoid the slightest whiff of scandal over Victoria and Lord Melbourne, the names of a number of possible husbands were put forward. The front runners were: the Duke of Cambridge and a prince of Saxe-Coburg in Germany. George, Duke of Cambridge had a number of severe disadvantages from the start. Quite apart from having even bushier sideburns than was fashionable – and that means bushy – in order to hide his bad complexion, Lord Melbourne didn't like him. So he had little chance . . . so that left Albert, Prince of Saxe-Coburg. He and Victoria were cousins and they'd already met when they were both seventeen. Victoria had thought that young Albert was very handsome.

VICTORIA AND ALBERT – THE EARLY YEARS

A date was set for Queen Victoria and Prince Albert to meet, to see how they got on and – er – possibly agree to marry. That date was 10 October 1839. The day didn't start too well. Victoria and Melbourne woke up with mild food poisoning from pork they'd eaten the night before, while poor Prince Albert was recovering from being seasick on the ferry crossing to England. 10 October 1839 was also the day that a nutter decided to break a lot of the windows at Windsor Castle ... but the actual meeting between the prince and the queen was a rip-roaring success.

A ROYAL PROPOSAL

It soon became obvious that Albert was as interested in Victoria as she was in him. All their meetings over those first few days had to be very formal and dignified. There was no holding of hands, and certainly no kissing (not even on the cheek). They did, however, get to shake hands when parting. On the third day, Prince Albert gave her hand an extra little squeeze when shaking it good night. The following day, 13 October 1839 they became engaged. (She asked him to marry her, because she was a queen, wasn't she? There was no way that *he* could have asked *her*.)

TITLE TROUBLE

The next thing that needed sorting was Albert's title. What should the Queen of Great Britain's husband be called? 'King' didn't seem right, because it would make him sound more important than her, and the public wouldn't stand for that. Victoria herself came up with the suggestion 'King Consort'. A 'consort' is a companion, so this would be like saying 'He's-king-because-he's-married-to-me-so-I'm-still-the-more-important-one-and-not-the-other-way-around', but no one thought that was a very good idea either. Some people even described Albert as 'a paper Royal Highness' which was a bit rude. It was like saying that he wasn't proper royalty. In the end, Albert, Prince of Saxe-Coburg simply stayed Albert, Prince of Saxe-Coburg ... but, one day, this would change.

A MEAN TRICK

Parliament paid Queen Victoria £385,000 a year for life. (Parliament had, in turn, got the money from people's taxes.) This sounds a huge amount because it was, but she

25

had to use it to pay for all her households, staff and expenses. When this was done, she was left with about £68,000, plus money she earned from other sources. When she married Albert, she expected him to be awarded £50,000 a year by parliament. This was the going rate for husbands or wives of members of the royal family. Instead, they voted to give him 'just' £30,000. Victoria was furious until Lord Melbourne pointed out that £30,000 would seem a lifetime's fortune to most people in a country full of poverty and unemployment. She had to accept the snub.

POOR OLD BRITAIN

Times were tough for ordinary people in early Victorian Britain. The 1840s became known as 'the Hungry Forties', with many people sick, homeless, out of work and starving. There were outbreaks of fever in the big cities. Some newspapers liked to contrast the horrible conditions of the people with the lavish luxury and comfort of the palace. It became important for the royal family to be seen to be supporting British workers by 'buying British'. At one royal christening, all the ladies were instructed to wear Paisley shawls and English lace.

WEDDING DAY BLISS

Unlike her coronation, Victoria's wedding went without a hitch. It took place on 10 February 1840 at the Chapel Royal, St James's, which was only a short ride from the palace. She was dressed in a white satin dress trimmed with lace, a diamond necklace and a sapphire brooch (from Albert) and an orange blossom wreath on her head. After the wedding ceremony, Victoria and Albert had a huge wedding breakfast (even though it was in the afternoon) at Buckingham Palace, then set off for Windsor Castle.

Well-wishers on horseback or in carriages rode up beside the royal newly-weds and wished them well. Albert settled down to play the piano while Victoria lay on the sofa with a terrible headache! Despite this, she wrote that she had feelings of 'heavenly love and happiness'. Victoria may have been Queen of Great Britain but, when it came to home life, it was Prince Albert who was very much in charge.

ATTACK IN THE PARK

When Albert threw his arms around Victoria, in the back of their open carriage on 10 June 1840, it wasn't to give her a loving hug. A man named Edward Oxford had just fired a pistol at the queen and was about to take another pot-shot. The carriage was on the way up Constitution Hill, greeted by cheering crowds. Victoria ducked to avoid the second bullet, while a bystander seized the would-be assassin to the cries of 'Kill him! Kill him!' from the on-lookers. This hero, a Mr Millais, had been cheering the queen with his son, John Everett Millais. The boy grew up to become a very well-known artist. Edward Oxford, meanwhile, spent 27 years in a lunatic asylum before emigrating. He was lucky. The penalty for treason was death.

OH LOOK, ALBERT! IS THAT ONE OF THOSE NEW-FANGLED CAMERAS?

THE FIRST OF MANY

Victoria and Albert's first child was born on 21 November 1840. She was a girl. When told by the doctor that it was a princess, Victoria replied, 'Never mind. The next will be a prince.' In those days, a prince was in line for the throne before a princess, even if he was born after her. (Nobody says life has to be fair.) The girl was named Victoria, after her mother and grandmother, and was given the title 'The Princess Royal'.

THE PRINCESS ROYAL

Although christened 'Victoria Adelaide Mary Louise', Queen Victoria used to call her 'the Child' then, a little later, 'Pussy' or 'Pussette' and, finally, 'Vicky'. Victoria left others to look after the princess, and thought her daughter was an ugly little thing – 'frog-like', even! When the princess grew up, she married the Emperor of Germany and they had a son, later referred to as Kaiser Bill. Kaiser Bill dragged Europe into the First World War, in which over ten million people died . . . but we're still in 1840, so these events were a long, long way off.

THE GRANDMOTHER OF EUROPE

In later life, Queen Victoria became known as the 'Grandmother of Europe'. She had nine children and LOADS of grandchildren, many of whom ended up on (or near!) the thrones of Europe. The heir to Great Britain's throne was Victoria and Albert's second child, Prince Edward, known as Bertie. He was born in 1841 and became the Prince of Wales. One day he would become King Edward VII. Four more sisters (Alice, Helena, Louise and Beatrice) and three brothers (Alfred, Arthur and Leopold) were to follow. Beatrice was the baby of the family, born in 1857.

THE CHRISTMAS TREE

Prince Albert is famous for having introduced the idea of the Christmas tree to Britain. Now, it's almost impossible to imagine

Christmas without one. It was in 1841 that Albert first ordered one from Coburg, and Victoria thought it was a wonderful idea. The truth be told, Queen Charlotte (wife of George III) had already had a Christmas tree at Windsor Castle in the 1790s, but it was Victoria's Albert who made them so fashionable and popular.

THE BOY JONES

At 1.30 a.m. on the morning of 3 December 1840 another boy came into Victoria's life. The queen's nurse was woken by the sound of someone opening the door that connected her bedroom to Queen Victoria's dressing-room. The nurse leapt up, bolted it shut and got help. Inside the queen's dressing-room, they found a boy hiding behind the sofa. Named Jones, it turned out that this was the second time he'd sneaked into the palace. The first time had been in 1838. He wasn't there to harm the queen. He was a fan! After a spell in prison, the Boy Jones (as he became known) managed to get into the palace a THIRD time. Once caught, he was sent away to sea.

A NEW PRIME MINISTER

In 1841, a new prime minister was elected. Lord Melbourne was out and Sir Robert Peel was in. Peel had been prime minister before, but not in Victoria's reign. There were two main political parties in those days: the Whigs and the Tories. Melbourne was a Whig who behaved like a Tory, and Peel was a Tory who behaved like a Whig. Clear so far? Jolly good. Peel didn't get on too well with Queen Victoria but got on fine with Albert. Peel created the police force, which is why the nickname for policemen (there were no policewomen back then) was 'Peelers'. During the time Peel was prime minister, Britain grew richer and life got a little easier for ordinary people.

NEW BROOM SWEEPS CLEAN

At Buckingham Palace, meanwhile, money was being wasted in enormous amounts, and everything seemed badly organized. Often, guests would get lost trying to find their rooms, meals would be late, and things were done in an odd way simply because that was the way they'd always been done. For example, it was the Lord Steward's job to make up a fire in the morning room, but not his job to light it. That was down to the Lord Chamberlain so, if they weren't both around at the same time, the fire didn't get lit and everyone got cold! Equally crazy was the way windows were cleaned. The job of cleaning them on the outside was left to the Department of Woods and Forests. The inside of the windows were left to the Lord Chamberlain. If they weren't done at the same time, the windows were never clean on both sides! In 1842, Albert was put in charge of trying to sort this mess out. The prince hired and fired staff and introduced simpler – and far more sensible – ways of doing things.

TWO MORE ATTACKS

Later that same year (and, for those of you not paying attention, that was 1842), there were three more attempts to kill Victoria, two by a man called John Francis, described by Albert as an 'ill-looking rascal'. His first attempt failed on 29 May, when his pistols misfired as he tried to shoot the queen in her carriage as she went down the Mall. Not wanting to risk becoming prisoners in their own home, Albert and Victoria decided not to tell the royal household and went out as usual the very next day! Surprise, surprise, Francis was waiting for them, fired, missed and was captured. Then, on 3 July, a boy called John William Bean tried shooting Victoria. Fortunately for her, the pistol contained more tobacco and paper than gunpowder (don't ask me why), and she was unharmed!

A CARING QUEEN

Victoria cared very much about her loyal subjects and became involved in individual cases. (There was no way she could help EVERYONE!) She listened to the concerns of the prison reformer Elizabeth Fry who did so much to improve conditions for prisoners in the nation's terrible jails. Victoria also hated the spectacle of public executions as a fun day out, gave money to families when she learnt of particular hardships . . . and was even worried about the welfare of a dwarf who used to entertain her at the palace!

FAT PROFITS, THIN FOLK

One of prime minister Robert Peel's great ambitions was to repeal the Corn Laws, which sounds pretty boring if you don't know what the Corn Laws were in the first place, or what 'repeal' means. The Corn Laws put such a big tax on any foreign corn brought into Britain that it was too expensive to be worth buying . . . so everyone had to buy British corn instead. The result? British farmers could charge as much as they liked for their crops, and make a big fat profit. And why was this such a big deal? Because corn made bread and, for many people, bread was about all they ever got to eat. Peel wanted to repeal these laws . . . and 'repeal' means to 'to revoke' or 'get rid of'. The Corn Laws were finally scrapped in June 1846 (a month after Victoria had given birth to Princess Helena). At the same time, Sir Robert Peel lost the post of prime minister to Lord Russell.

THE STARVING IRISH

In Ireland, which was a single colony under British rule at that time, at least half the people didn't live off bread but off potatoes. In 1845, the Irish potato crop was diseased and many people went hungry. The following year, the potatoes went black and died. In 1847, there was another disastrous crop. From a population of about eight million people, over one and a half million died and another one and a half million people emigrated to countries such as America, meaning Ireland lost almost 40 per cent of its people. Victoria had wanted to visit Ireland on a number of occasions but it was only deemed 'safe' in 1849. She thought the women were beautiful but wondered why they wore rags.

MORE ATTEMPTS ON HER LIFE

On 19 May 1849, before her trip to Ireland, Queen Victoria was shot at by someone later described as being 'a mad Irishman'. His name was William Hamilton and he borrowed the gun from his landlady. He wasn't really aiming at the queen. He simply wanted to give her a bit of a fright. Hamilton had tried to create a home-made pistol with a teapot spout for the barrel but had failed . . . what bothered Victoria was that he'd been Irish, not that he was mad. She was beginning to wonder just how welcome she'd be in Ireland. Just over a year later, on 27 June 1850, she was hit over the head by a retired lieutenant called Robert Pate. But he was *English*, so that was all right then! Despite being knocked out, she went to the opera in the evening and received a heroine's welcome from the audience. Less than a week later, Sir Robert Peel died from a fall from his horse.

THE SCOTTISH RETREAT

Victoria first visited the get-away-from-it-all castle of Balmoral in September 1848. She and Albert fell in love with the place at once. Hidden away in the Scottish Highlands, it was peaceful and free from prying eyes. She found the Scottish servants loyal and attentive, if not brilliant at their jobs. What disappointed her more, though, was that the Scots didn't look very Scottish. None wore a kilt, for a start! Soon the royal family were looking more 'Scottish' than the Scots. Albert and the children wore kilts and the queen wore tartan! They returned the following year, armed with a Scottish dictionary, and took Scottish dancing lessons. Victoria was hooked, and soon all things Scottish became very fashionable indeed.

THE GREAT EXHIBITION AND ALBERT'S LAST TEN YEARS

In January 1850, Prince Albert chaired the first meeting of the Commissioners for the Great Exhibition, which he wanted to open the following year. The idea was for Britain to hold a festival celebrating ideas and inventions from all around the world. It would be a show case for Victorian achievement, housed in a fantastic 'crystal palace'. The building was to be designed by Joseph Paxton and would like an absolutely enormous conservatory. It was a brilliant and far-sighted idea but, because he was an unpopular foreigner and a 'paper Royal Highness', Parliament wouldn't give him any funds. Albert was so sure of the success of his scheme that he went ahead without government backing.

PLANS PLEASE

Joseph Paxton's plans were just one of 234 submitted in a competition to design the building. Paxton wasn't an architect but a gardener! He worked for the Duke of Devonshire and had designed the greenhouses at the Duke's grand house, Chatsworth. Albert was impressed with Paxton's plans, had seen the greenhouses and thought that a 'crystal palace' would be a fantastic building to house the Exhibition. Now it was all systems go.

I THINK THE IDEA OF A GIANT GREENHOUSE IS BRILLIANT, PAXTON. BUT WHERE WILL WE GET THE GIANT VEGETABLES TO GO IN IT?

ON A GRAND SCALE

Hyde Park in London was chosen as the site for the Crystal Palace. The Palace was a HUGE structure, big enough to house mature trees. The world had never seen anything like it! It was made of 4,572 tonnes of iron and about 300,000 pains of glass. It was 564 metres long and covered about 4 square kilometres. There were even 24 MILES of guttering! Queen Victoria was a little worried that it might be damaged by hail stones . . . part of the conservatory at Buckingham Palace had been, and she hated the idea of glass falling in on the visitors!

BOTHERSOME BIRDS

The problem with having a building big enough to house full-grown trees was that the Crystal Palace would also house the thousands of birds that roosted in them. The birds were a nuisance in many ways, but the worst thing about them was the noise they made and the droppings they left everywhere. But how to get rid of them? You couldn't shoot them because you'd shatter the glass! It was the world famous general, the Duke of Wellington, hero of the Battle of Waterloo, who came up with the solution. 'Try sparrowhawks, ma'am,' he said to Victoria.

WHAT'S IN STORE

There were over 14,000 exhibits from all over the world, divided into different sections. These were: Raw Materials, Mechanical Inventions, Manufacturers and Works of Art. The Exhibition was packed with some of the latest inventions from around the world, from the brilliant to the bizarre. There was everything from the electric telegraph, which could send messages over amazing distances, to a telescope coffin, which could be adjusted to fit the size of the body! The motto of the Great Exhibition, written on the official catalogue, read: *The Earth is the Lord's and all that therein is.*

THE GRAND OPENING

The Great Exhibition officially opened its doors on 1 May 1851. It was a sunny day. Of course it would be; Queen Victoria was there and sunshine was the Queen's Weather. She arrived in an open carriage, dressed in pink and silver with feathers, and wore the stunning Koh-i-Noor diamond. As she walked up the aisle of the cathedral-like Crystal Palace, organ after organ burst into music as she passed each one. Anywhere else this would have been deafening. In the vast space of the Crystal Palace, however, she later said that she could hardly hear them!

THE KOH-I-NOOR DIAMOND

'Koh-i-Noor' means 'Mountain of Light' in Persian, and this enormous diamond had changed hands lots of times between rulers of the Indian sub-continent before being presented to Queen Victoria in 1849. When Victoria was made Empress of India, amongst all her other titles, the Koh-i-Noor was set in the royal crown. It's now one of the most famous of the Crown Jewels. This has caused some confusion because India itself became known as 'the jewel in the crown'.

NOT WHAT HE SEEMED

Amongst the members of the Diplomatic Corps at the grand opening ceremony was a most impressive-looking Chinese man called He Sing. He even appears in an official painting of the

Exhibition, wearing a blue tunic, gold necklaces and fan. The strange thing about He Sing, though, is that he wasn't a diplomat at all. Mr He Sing was the captain of a junk (a Chinese sailing ship) moored on the Thames and he made his money by charging Londoners a shilling each to look around it! He'd somehow got mixed up in the procession with the Diplomatic Corps and, realizing that he was on to a good thing, decided to go along with it!

A SENSATIONAL SUCCESS

When the doors to the Great Exhibition closed for the final time on 15 October 1851, over six million paying visitors had passed through them. Queen Victoria had been a regular visitor, visiting it nearly every day from its opening right up until July. Prince Albert's dream had become a sensational reality and made a mind-boggling profit of nearly a quarter of a million pounds! There had been those who'd thought that the whole idea had been doomed to failure from the start. Parliament hadn't even been willing to put up a penny to fund it, fearing that it would lose money! No one could deny Albert his hour of glory now. The queen described it as the happiest and proudest day of her life.

ON THE MOVE

The Crystal Place wasn't demolished but taken down piece by piece so that it could be re-erected on a new site in 1854. The site chosen was Sydenham Hill in South London, but the area was renamed Crystal Palace and is still called that today. (If there hadn't been the Great Exhibition, there would never have been a Crystal Palace Football Club. Whether that's a good thing or a bad thing is a matter of opinion.) The Palace itself was destroyed in a terrible fire in 1936 and none of the main structure remains. There are, however, still some rather strange stone dinosaurs lurking in what were once its grounds.

A NEW TITLE FOR ALBERT?

In 1852, not long before his own death, the Duke of Wellington offered Albert the important job of being Commander-in-Chief of the British Army. This was a great honour, but the prince said 'no', wanting to be able to devote more time to the queen. In 1857, however, an act of parliament was passed to give him a new title. He became Prince Consort. This gave Albert an official role in British life alongside Victoria, rather than him just being a prince of some funny-sounding German place.

A WHOLE RAFT OF PRIME MINISTERS

During the 1850s, Queen Victoria saw a whole load of prime ministers come and go! There was Lord Russell, the Earl of Derby (twice), Lord Aberdeen and, finally, Lord Palmerston, who she saw through until 1865 . . . her most famous prime ministers, Benjamin Disraeli and William Gladstone were yet to come, so you'll just have to wait! It was also during the 1850s that Britain fought a war alongside the French rather than against them, which was pretty unusual. This was the Crimean War and led to the fame of another legendary female figure: Florence Nightingale.

FLORENCE NIGHTINGALE

Victoria is famous for saying that women weren't fit to govern, which was rather odd because she was doing such a good job herself! She was also an avid supporter of another strong-willed

woman, named Florence Nightingale. Called 'The Lady with the Lamp', Florence became famous for championing the cause of proper nursing at home and abroad. In 1854 the Crimean War broke out, with the British and the French fighting alongside the Turks against the Russians. There were many bloody battles and thousands were dying on all sides. Florence and a small band of British nurses went over to Turkey and the Crimea to work in army hospitals. The queen and Florence met after the war in 1856.

LIKE WOW!

Victoria benefited from an experimental new medical procedure when she gave birth to her son Leopold in 1853. Her pain was eased by being given chloroform. This anaesthetic was first tested in 1847, and was given to the queen by a famous anaesthetist from Edinburgh called Dr John Snow. This had been the idea of Sir James Clark, Victoria's fresh-air fanatic doctor, which only goes to show that even an oddball can have a good idea once in a while. Queen Victoria became a huge fan of 'blessed chloroform' forever after, making it popular with the people (that's ordinary folk, like you and me).

THE ROYAL DISEASE

Sadly, Prince Leopold was born with haemophilia, a disease which stops your blood from clotting, so a single untreated cut can kill you. Only men can get the disease which isn't 'caught' but passed on through the mother who, herself, is perfectly healthy. This meant that Victoria's daughters had the haemophilia gene and could pass it on to any male children they had. In this way – Victoria ended up with forty grandchildren – haemophilia was spread throughout the royal families of Europe.

VICTORIA CROSS

In 1856, Victoria created a new medal, the Victoria Cross, sometimes called the VC. Given 'For Valour' this became – and still is – the highest British military decoration. The first Victoria Crosses were awarded to British soldiers fighting in the Crimean War. They were made from the melted-down metal of captured Russian guns.

SAD NEWS

On 16 March 1861, Victoria's mother, the Duchess of Kent died and, despite the fact that the woman had driven Victoria bonkers for much of her life, the queen was heartbroken. She became quite irritable and went into mourning. Rumours were now spreading that she was either mad, going mad, or was very ill. It didn't help that Prince Albert had had a nasty riding accident so wasn't in any real condition to comfort her.

THE END

Prince Albert did all he could to cheer Victoria up but, sadly, as she got better, he got worse. Like so many other members of the royal families of Europe, Albert had gone and caught typhoid. On Friday 22 November 1861, he came back soaking wet having inspected the military Staff College at Sandhurst in the rain. He thought he'd caught a chill . . . actually, it was the death of him. He died on Saturday 14 December, clasping his beloved Victoria's hand. The queen's life would never be the same again.

AFTER ALBERT

Albert had been the love of Queen Victoria's life, and now he was gone. Without him, life just didn't seem worth living. Victoria was 44-years-old and, little did she realize, she had another 40 years to live. She had Albert buried beneath a white marble statue in a mausoleum in the grounds of Windsor Castle. She only visited it twice a year – his birthday and at Christmas – but he was always in her thoughts.

A LITTLE OFF HER ROCKER?

Although now a widow, Victoria still kept two visitors' books at her royal residences: one for her and one for dead Albert . . . and everyone was expected to solemnly sign both of them. Nobody dared point out that it was a bit odd! She also took to carrying a photograph of Albert, not so that she could look at his picture but so that she could 'show' Albert's photo all the sights she was seeing!

AND THAT'S NOT ALL

Not only did Victoria wear black, which was usual for a grieving widow, but she expected everyone else to wear black too. Not just her servants and her officials. Everyone. The whole country should be in mourning . . . Not that she'd have known whether they were or not. She didn't attend a public engagement for two years. People were beginning to forget what she looked like. There were rumblings of discontent. What was the point of spending all that money on a queen if she never even showed her face?

LIFE GOES ON AND ON AND ON . . .

Just because Albert was dead and buried didn't mean that his clothes shouldn't be laid out for him every day. At least, that's what Victoria thought, and no one dared argue with her. She also instructed that Albert's chamber pot be taken from under the bed each morning and given a thoroughly good scrub . . . not that it was terribly likely the dead prince would have used it.

THE ALBERT MEMORIAL

The queen encouraged towns and villages to erect statues of Albert all over the country. She chose to have her own memorial to him put up in Hyde Park, the site of his greatest triumph, the Great Exhibition. It shows Albert seated under a very fancy stone canopy. (The statue itself was gilded – covered in gold – but, during the Second World War was painted black so that it wouldn't glint in the moonlight and become a target for bombers. It's now been restored to its former glinting glory.) Later, a number of public buildings relating to Albert's interests were built nearby: the Royal Albert Hall, the Victoria and Albert Museum and the Science Museum. They're all still there today.

JOHN BROWN

One man is given more credit for getting Victoria back into public life than any other and he is John Brown. He's also credited as having brought disgrace to himself and the queen. John Brown had been Albert's favourite 'gillie' – gentleman servant – at Balmoral. He drank too much, smoked too much, was plain-speaking and often spoke his mind. He was different to the other servants and, perhaps, that's why Victoria took a shine to him. She had Brown move down to Windsor Castle and gave him the title 'The Queen's Highland Servant'. Because no one had had that title before, no one quite knew who could tell him what to do!

MRS BROWN

In the same way that the young Victoria had earned the nickname Mrs Melbourne, all the way back on page 20, now the gossips were calling her 'Mrs Brown'. John Brown didn't speak to her like she was his queen, but as though she was his *wife*. There were even rumours that they got drunk together, which might have happened. In the end, he simply seems to have outlived his usefulness and, once the queen was back in public life, wasn't so important to her. But that wasn't strictly true.

A TERRIBLE YEAR

In 1871, Victoria was ill. By now she was almost as wide as she was tall and – being under five feet tall – must have been quite an unusual sight. Still shunning public appearances, she was troubled by her arm. Sometimes it was painful and sometimes she lost feeling in it. She also lost two stone in weight. Worse still, just as the tenth anniversary of Albert's death from typhoid approached, Victoria's son and heir, 'Bertie' the Prince of Wales, caught typhoid too.

AT DEATH'S DOOR

The telegram announcing Bertie's feverish attack reached the queen on 21 November. The news that it was typhoid, but only a mild form, reached her on 22 November. When news reached her that it was far from mild and that her son was now delirious, with a high temperature, she hurried to be with him. As 14 December drew nearer and nearer – the anniversary of Albert's death – a terrible gloom descended on Victoria, she was convinced that Bertie would die too. The day came, and the prince was suddenly feeling better. He went on to make a full recovery.

PUBLIC JOY

The Prince of Wales wasn't the most popular person with the public, but his illness had captured their imagination. Many felt sorry for Victoria having lost Albert. Now what if she lost her son and heir? They sent the queen messages of sympathy. When the news broke that he had recovered, there was much public rejoicing. There was a Service of Thanksgiving at St Paul's Cathedral on 27 February 1872, which Victoria attended in person.

BROWN TO THE RESCUE!

Two days later, another apparent attempt was made on Victoria's life – the first one in quite a while! A youth called Arthur O'Connor pointed a pistol at the queen as she passed by in her carriage. Prince Arthur, travelling with his mother, leapt out of the carriage to try to tackle the attacker, but John Brown got there first. As a result, Brown got all the thanks and credit, along with a gold medal and £25 a year for life. This annoyed Arthur, who thought he'd been just as brave. As it was, it turned out that O'Connor's pistol wasn't even loaded. He'd simply wanted to draw attention to the troubles in Ireland and wanted Fenian prisoners released. After a year in prison, he agreed to be transported abroad, as long as it was to somewhere with nice weather.

HERE WE GO AGAIN

Events on 2 March 1882 caused Queen Victoria to remark, 'It is worth being shot at to see how much one is loved.' A man called Roderick McLean had shot at the queen's carriage as it waited at the front of Windsor railway station. Although John Brown was present, two Eton schoolboys were the heroes of the day. They attacked Mr McLean with umbrellas until he was arrested and dragged away. While we're on the subject of assassination attempts and umbrellas, it's reported that Victoria carried a chain mail lined parasol for a while, to shield herself from would-be assassins' bullets!

LIVING ON IN DEATH

John Brown died in 1883, having caught a chill whilst on the queen's business – looking into the mysterious affair of an alleged attack on the writer and traveller Lady Florence

Dixie, supposedly by two men dressed as women! On hearing the news of his death, Victoria ordered that his room at Windsor be left exactly as it was, except for a fresh flower to be placed on his pillow every morning. A statue of John Brown was put up at Balmoral.

GLADSTONE AND DISRAELI

Two other men who'd become a big part of the queen's life were the two prime ministers Benjamin Disraeli and William Gladstone, who, between them, led the British Government for much of the time from 1868 right up until 1894 – with just a small gap, filled by the Marquis of Salisbury, in between. Victoria was a big fan of Disraeli's and the two got on really well. As far as her relationship with Gladstone went, she found him a real BORE!

DIZZY AND GLADSTONE

Benjamin Disraeli, nicknamed 'Dizzy', led the Tory party. He loved wearing flashy clothes. (He was famous for his gaudy waistcoats.) He dyed his hair black and had a little goatee beard – at a time when many important Victorians had HUGE bushy beards. As well as being a politician, he also wrote novels. He was prime minister twice. Gladstone was Whig, a Member of Parliament for 61 years and had the nickname GOM (which was short for Grand Old Man). He didn't have a beard at all, but that didn't stop him being prime minister four times.

HOME AND AWAY

Disraeli was interested in the British Empire. As far as he was concerned, the bigger it was the better. It was thanks to him that Victoria was able to add Empress of India to her many titles, and you can be sure that she liked him even more for it. He even arranged for Britain to buy (most of) the Suez Canal, an important shipping lane that plenty of countries would have liked to have laid their hands on. Gladstone, however, was no Empire builder. In fact, he was eager to give Ireland – all still a British colony then, remember – back to the Irish in his Home Rule bill.

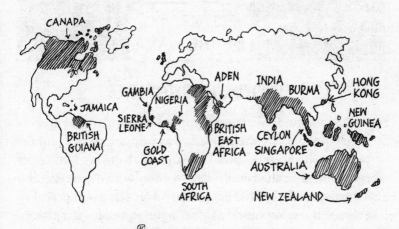

THE BRITISH EMPIRE

Much of the world map was printed in red at the height of Queen Victoria's power, because red meant that it was a part of the British Empire. These were the parts of the world 'owned' and governed by the British, usually taken by force. So large in Victoria's day, it was said, 'the sun never sets on the British

Empire'. In other words, Britain had so much territory around the globe, you could guarantee that at least one part of it was in daylight, whatever time of day or night it was back in Britain.

IMPROVING EVERYDAY LIVES

Both Disraeli and Gladstone wanted to improve the lives of ordinary people. Disraeli passed laws doubling the number of people who were allowed to vote in elections (although, as was typical at the time, none of these was a woman). He also introduced the Public Health Act, leading to greatly improved living conditions for many people. Gladstone tried to cut tax where he could and make life easier for the people of the new industrial middle classes.

THE INDUSTRIAL AGE

Britain and the world changed almost beyond recognition during Victoria's reign. If I tried to list the amazing inventions and advances that were made during this time, there'd have been no room for anything about Victoria's own life in this book! Factories sprang up everywhere, railway tracks opened up whole continents, steamships crossed the oceans, even the first cars – called 'horseless carriages' – were invented. The plus side was that these new factories and machines could feed, clothe and supply the millions of people in the British Empire. The minus side was that machines could put people out of work.

BACK WITH A BANG

After years of wearing black, hiding from the public, not being a very good monarch and being a general misery guts, Victoria came back into public life with a bang. It was 1887 and she'd been on the throne for fifty years. It was agreed that there'd be Golden Jubilee celebrations across the land, throughout the Empire even, and she reluctantly agreed to be a part of them. There were street parties, fancy balls, parades, fireworks displays – you name it, it happened – wild celebrations and loads and loads of especially made souvenirs from biscuit tins to porcelain. 30,000 school children in Hyde Park were each given a bun, some milk and a Jubilee mug. Victoria ended up having a great time!

THE MUNSHI

It was in this year that another servant came to mean a great deal to Queen Victoria. He was 24 year-old Abdul Karim, from India. His father was a doctor and in his own country, Abdul had been a Munshi – a clerk – which was a well-respected job back home, so he objected to being a mere servant. Victoria admired him for it and started taking him everywhere with her, and the palace officials soon came to loath him. Beginning to sound familiar, huh? He even tried to teach Victoria Hindustani.

THE DIAMOND JUBILEE

Victoria's Golden Jubilee had been such a success that, when 1897 came around, she decided to hold Diamond (60-year) Jubilee celebrations. When, on 22 June she rode out in her carriage – still dressed in black mind you, and clasping a black parasol – she had never been so popular. It was unlikely any British monarch could have been *more* popular. She was adored by the thousands there and the millions who were holding their own celebrations elsewhere.

DEATH AND WAR

Victoria's son Bertie had cheated death, but Prince Alfred was not so lucky. He died in February 1900 and was buried on 10 February, 60 years to the day since Victoria had married Albert. On 11 October, the second Boer War broke out in Africa. The queen was sent telegrams to keep her up to date with developments and regularly reviewed troops and visited hospitals. She even arranged for 100,000 tins of chocolate to be distributed amongst regular soldiers (but not the officers, who'd hogged other presents in the past).

THE END DRAWS NEAR

Queen Victoria's last public engagement was at the Irish Industries Exhibition in Windsor, in December 1900. Victoria had become fond of the Irish, after the bravery of Irish troops in the Boer War. She had created a new regiment of Irish Guards and had visited Ireland in April (being steered clear of places with strong anti-British feelings). That same December, the queen left Windsor Castle for the last time and went to Osborne, a house on the Isle of Wight in which she'd first stayed with her family way back in 1844.

AROUND THE BED

Queen Victoria died at Osborne on Monday 22 January 1901. Some say her that the last thing she said was 'Bertie,' others, more romantically perhaps, say that she sighed, 'Oh, Albert . . .' On her bed for much of the time had been Turi, a little Pomeranian dog. Around her bed stood her children and grandchildren. The house itself was surrounded by police to stop the news of the queen's death leaking out before the prime minister had been told. Then a short statement was read out at the gates: 'Her majesty the Queen breathed her last at 6.30 p.m., surrounded by her children and grandchildren.' Her record-breaking 63-and-a-bit-year reign was over. Reporters leapt onto their bikes and peddled frantically into town to telephone their newspapers.

FROM BLACK TO WHITE

Victoria had left strict instructions about her own funeral. After all her years of wearing black in mourning, it was to be an all-white affair. She was dressed in a white dress, with a lace veil from her wedding day, and placed in her coffin along with photos – the one of John Brown hidden by flowers – a plaster cast of Albert's hand (they used to give them as presents to each other!) and his old dressing-gown . . . Yup, you read that right the first time: Albert's dressing-gown.

A TECHNICAL HITCH

The royal yacht *Alberta* carried the coffin from the Isle of White to Portsmouth where it was put on a train to Paddington Station in London. Wherever the train passed, people took off their hats or knelt down. The coffin was then transferred to another train and taken to Windsor. Here, it was placed on a gun carriage pulled by horses, and a procession began to make its way towards Windsor Castle ... but, horror of horrors, the horses pulling the coffin broke the harness.

THE NAVY TO THE RESCUE

As quick as a flash, the broken harness was replaced with either telephone cable or the communication cord from the train, and the horses were replaced with a bunch of burly sailors from the procession. They then heaved Queen Victoria all the way up to St George's Chapel in the castle!

BACK WITH BELOVED ALBERT

Days later, Victoria's coffin was taken to the mausoleum where Albert's body already lay. The public funeral was over. This was a family affair. Now Victoria's white marble statue could be put beside Albert's . . . though there were a nasty few days when no one could find it. It'd been put away for safe keeping and, as so often happens when someone does that, it was very difficult to find. Finally, it was tracked down to an alcove in a wall of the castle. As the family left the mausoleum, there was snow. This certainly wasn't typical Queen's Weather, but this did give Victoria the white funeral she'd hoped for.

HER NAME LIVES ON

The Victorian era saw so many changes that it is seen in many ways as a 'golden age' of world history – despite some of the terrible things done in the name of 'Empire'. This was a time when the whole world was 'opened up' by explorers from the west, science gave up some incredible secrets and machines changed the way most things were done. Victoria herself gave her name to everything from an African waterfall and a London railway station to a state in Australia, and plenty more besides.

WE ARE NOT AMUSED

So, now that we're at the end of Victoria's long life and reign, tinged with sadness throughout, I suppose we can see why she had reason not to be amused *all* of the time. As a teenager, she'd attended a lecture on alchemy (the pseudo-science of trying to turn base metal into gold) and had reported that she was 'very MUCH amused'. When writing about dancing, she claimed to be 'VERY much amused', but it's for this one phrase about NOT being amused that she's remembered. It's not fair really, is it? Some people imagine she never even smiled, but I've seen a photo of her with a big cheesy grin on her face, so that can't be true now, can it? She was only human, after all, and a pretty remarkable human at that!

A FEW FAMOUS VICTORIANS

Queen Victoria had pretty much ruled the world for over sixty years during one of the most exciting times in history. This list could, therefore, be about a million pages long, but that would use up too many trees and harm the environment, so here are just a handful of famous Victorian folk:

Isambard Kingdom BRUNEL (1806-1859) Great name. Brilliant engineer. Built steamships, bridges, railways, tunnels, the lot. Most of them worked properly. Most of them.

Lewis CARROLL (1832-1898) Most famous for writing *Alice in Wonderland* and *Alice Through the Looking Glass*. Victoria so loved Alice that she asked Carroll to send any other books he'd written. She received *Syllabus of Plane Algebraical Geometry*. Carroll's real name was the Reverend Charles Lutwidge Dodgson and he was a mathematican!

Charles DARWIN (1809-1882) A biologist who wrote *Origin of Species*. In it, he argued that all life was descended from the same ancestors but had evolved in different ways. In other words, humans weren't descended from apes – which some people thought he was saying – but had the same ancestors as apes. These views upset those who thought God created everything as it is.

Charles DICKENS (1812-1870) One of Britain's most famous writers ever, probably second only to William Shakespeare. Many of his novels highlighted what he thought was wrong in the world, centring on the problems of the poor. Had a fabulous beard, even by Victorian standards.

General Charles George GORDON (1833-1885) A Victorian hero. After commanding his 'ever victorious army' which put down rebellions in China, he became Governor of Sudan. He was killed by the enemy after the ten month siege of Khartoum. Became known as 'Gordon of Khartoum'.

Jack the Ripper The most famous Victorian murderer, if not *the* most famous murderer of all time. A very nasty piece of work who murdered at least five women in London in 1888. No one knows his true identity. At one time, one of Queen Victoria's own grandsons was a suspect!

Rudyard KIPLING (1865-1936) Born in India, he became a megastar English writer at the end of the Victorian era and was a great believer in the British Empire. His most famous books today are probably the *Just So Stories* and *The Jungle Book*. He was a great fan of the common soldier.

David LIVINGSTONE (1813-1873) Scottish missionary and explorer. Believed that converting Africans to Christianity and trading with them might help to put a stop to the terrible slave trade. 'Discovered' many places, including the Victoria Falls (not that the locals didn't know they were there already!)

Alfred, Lord TENNYSON (1809-1902) Poet Laureate (the queen's official poet). Famous for writing long, narrative poems, including *The Charge of the Light Brigade* and *Idylls of the King. Idylls of the King* was a wildly romantic retelling of the legend of King Arthur.

OK, so they're all men and most of them had big beards, but that pretty much sums up famous Victorians for you!

TIMELINE

At home and abroad

1819	Victoria is born.
1838	Victoria's coronation.
1840	Victoria marries Albert.
	'Penny Post' introduced, with 'Penny Black' stamps.
1845-51	Irish Potato Famine.
1846	*Elias Howe invents the sewing machine.*
1849	*Walter Hunt invents the safety pin.*
1851	The Great Exhibition is held at the Crystal Palace in Hyde Park.
1853	*Pierre Carpentier invents corrugated iron.*
1854-56	Crimean War.
1861	Death of Albert, the Prince Consort.
1862	*Richard Gatling invents the machine gun.*
1864	The Albert Memorial is built.
1866	*Alfred Nobel invents dynamite.*
1871	*Stanley says to Livingstone, 'Dr Livingstone, I presume?'*
1875	*World's first phone call.*
1885	*General Gordon is killed at Khartoum.*
1887	Victoria's Golden Jubilee.
1888	*Jack the Ripper on the loose in London.*
1889	*The Eiffel Tower is erected in Paris.*
1893	*Britain's Labour Party founded.*
1895	*Gillette invents the safety razor.*
1897	Victoria's Diamond Jubilee.
1898	*Spanish-American War.*
1899-1902	(2nd) Boer War.
1901	Victoria dies.
	Hubert Booth invents the electric vacuum cleaner.